Sun Setting Over Victoria

The **Orage** Press

First published by the Orage Press in 2011 by
The Orage Press, 16a Heaton Road, Mitcham, Surrey, CR4 2BU, England

ISBN: 978-0-956580290

Printed in England by Lightning Source. Set in Baskerville

Part six of the New Aesthetics.

CLIVE HEAD

Sun Setting Over Victoria

The **Orage** Press

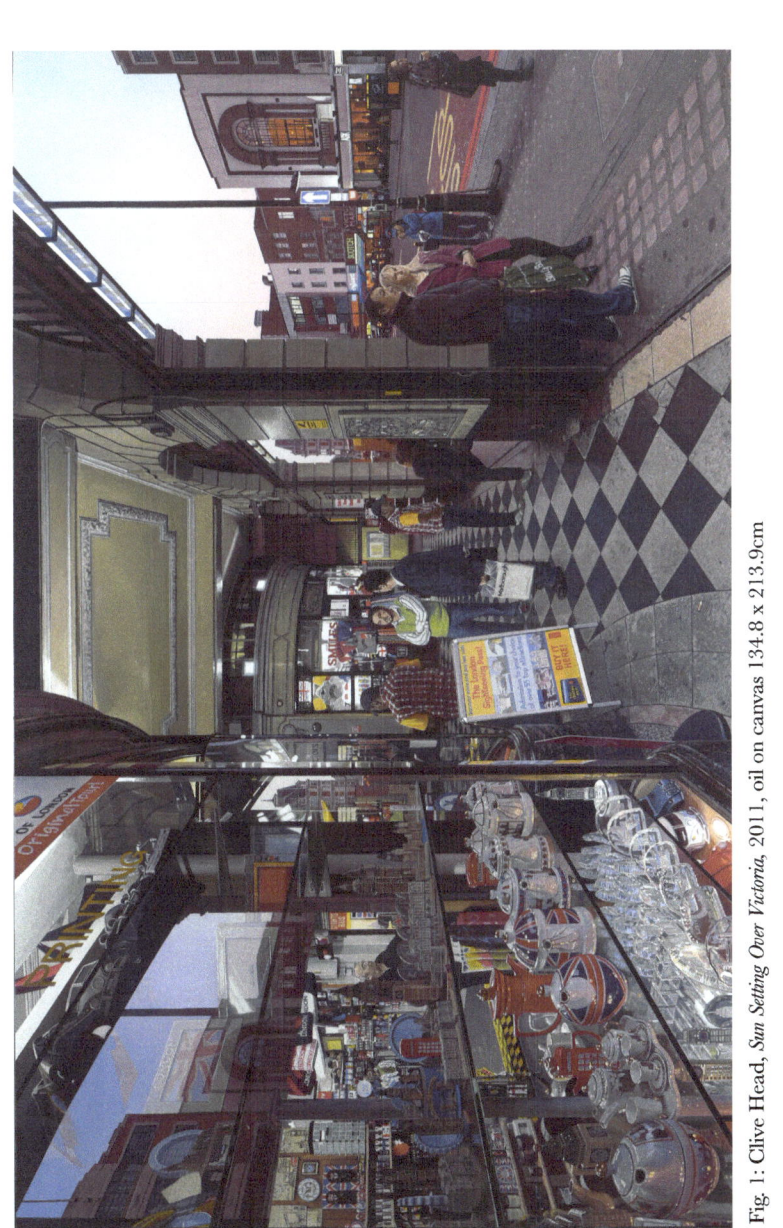

Fig. 1: Clive Head, *Sun Setting Over Victoria*, 2011, oil on canvas 134.8 x 213.9cm

This text is based on a lecture given at the University of Northampton in March 2011 to an audience of art students and lecturers. This looked back on my recent activities, notably my exhibition at the National Gallery, and the completion of a new painting.

Any account of my activities is going to be centred on me, so it seems imperative to state that I define an artist as someone who understands that art is autonomous. It has an absolute state and is not simply whatever an artist claims it to be. My responsibility is to understand the nature of art and how it functions and to use this knowledge to develop new possibilities within the framework of art. This centres art on its material manifestation, notably paintings, drawings and sculptures which exist independent of their makers. The state of being an artist is only applicable when the individual is engaged in the process of making a work of art, and only deserving if that work of art is believable.

This art-centric practice may well be at odds with the ego-centric practice of much contemporary activity inside the art world. But if our attentions are focussed on the artist and not the extraordinary nature of art itself, art inevitably results in servicing the artist as a performer, a personality and a politician. In this state art loses its independence, importance and objective quality. Too often we are left with inert things particularly when they are removed from the circus that surrounds the artist. In failing to understand the relationship between art and the artist we fail to understand the nature of art.

On this basis, the invitation to exhibit my work at the National Gallery last year was all the more challenging. My paintings had to hold their own. There could be no extraneous agendas to account for their deviation from being credible; no conceptualism outside of the framework of art to hide behind. The remarkable paintings in the National Gallery collection simply don't work in this way, they are clear and absolute and asked to be judged on their visual merit.

As a collection the National Gallery has effectively determined my understanding of art. I have been looking at it from my youth. Whereas the Tate often falters, confusing illustration with art, I rarely descend into thinking about social narratives or the ego of the maker when looking at paintings in the National. There is a shared understanding across the centuries that art, irrespective of its social, religious or political beginnings, must assert a credible reality that takes us out of our world, and there is always the fascination for me to see how this has been created. Recognising that art *functions* to create such extraordinary worlds and understanding how it functions defines the mechanics of its framework.

Whereas this might reject particular agendas from the notion of art (notably those underpinned by the import of semiotics into art history) I do not regard this as being restrictive. Clouding our minds with an expectation that art can offer us a narrative on our world often leads to a failure to recognise the astonishing alternative reality that an artist has invented. To engage with art at this profound level requires us to let go of the narrative ties that can hold us back. I am not advocating a modernist formal appreciation of art, which tends to reduce art to its material components, but a contemplation of how art transforms from everyday experience to creating an entire universe. In this, we are discussing infinite possibilities rooted in a faith in the existence of these worlds. This is a faith in art. What is being offered on the walls of the National Gallery is extraordinary experiences and a tool box for the development of painting in the future. Rejecting this understanding is truly limiting and has become a real danger in our modern world.

So it was important for me to stage an exhibition of works which highlighted the journey from experiencing our reality to the creation of alternative realities. To do this I made paintings based on quite unappealing locations in London which, if successful, would draw the viewer in and delight them. This establishes that art does not mimic our world, even though the subject may be familiar to us. It offers us a resolution to our world, fixing the chaos, flux and uncertainty. In short, the painting has made palatable all that is normally difficult to tolerate if the viewer elects to engage with the painting and takes comfort from this experience. Of course it would be unnatural for me to try to resolve the horror of a saint's martyrdom, as so many artists have done in the past, but the experience of being in the city is one that we can all relate to and from which we all at times wish to escape. Only art can offer this escape within representations of the very subject from which we seek refuge.

With the installation of the show in place it felt necessary for me to engage in the activity of being an artist once again, and to make a painting whilst exhibiting at the National. This took place in the privacy of the studio where indifference to everything apart from the demands of art is a necessary condition. But the painting must be rooted in experience, a physical and sensory engagement with the world. The point at which this experience starts and ceases, and the artwork begins is difficult to pin down. There were beginnings in my many visits to the area outside the entrances to Victoria Underground Station. I like its configuration of spaces, its mix of textures, its worn elegance, the individuals who run the shops and sell bus tour tickets, the ceaseless flow of people just passing through. I like all its colours and lights. I like the still-lifes in the windows, chequerboard floor and arches which put me in mind of so many paintings. But it is also a place that I happen to find myself in. It is an area where I have a history.

Before thinking about a painting, I need to experience a place without pre-conceiving how it could be painted. To seek a 'view' at the outset is to overlay a conceptual framework (the concept of a view) which would compromise the integrity of the raw sensory engagement. I may make some visual notes to deepen the engagement, not to distance myself from it. At this point it is essential that I am *not* being an artist, just a human being. Being in a place involves my movement around it over a period of time. I look at and touch different objects and surfaces, the relationship between which is determined by my presence within the space. Even at the point when I try to record some of this with a camera, there is no *pictorial* connection between all the different spaces, objects and people that have been witnessed.

The photography I use is fraught with problems, and I seem to be alighting on increasingly more difficult places and times of the day to attempt this documentary process. This is partly because of an ongoing commitment to making paintings which seek *explicitly* a resolution to the chaotic flux of the city. It is also partly a desire to deal with situations that are largely outside of what can successfully be recorded through a camera. But the greatest motivation is to elicit a sensory overload, the kind which is at odds with the contemplative process essential to making art. Being pushed around and confronted by people, being blocked by traffic, cautioned by police and in all this mayhem trying to record everything I see around me, above me, and in all directions as I move around, coupled with the technical difficulties of changing many films, dealing with depths of field, exposure, focus, there is no opportunity to be an artist and make art. This is an adrenalin fuelled experience after which I just have hundreds of transparencies. The action has taken place on the need to make art in the future. There isn't a predetermined pictorial concept. It is not a creative act, nor the actions of an artist. My presence, standing on the steps of a busy underground station in the rush hour adds to the chaos. The action of being an artist must happen later under very different conditions.

I use a medium format camera with a lens that is as near to being wide angle without getting too much barrel distortion. Maybe this goes back to when I cared a little about the nature of camera vision. I have used the same equipment for over a decade. The point here is that my photographs are not conventional close-ups. They are moderately wide-angled and are on the limits of photographic vision before it all gets very distorted. The photographs of Victoria illustrated in this essay *[figs. 2, 3 and 11]* are reproduced full-frame, but they only refer to small sections of the final painting. Irrespective of whatever lens I put on a camera it is not possible to take a photograph of what is finally presented in the painting. Several professional photographers have tried and failed because the world I *paint* only exists in the painting.

Standing in the arcade opposite the Tube entrance and turning to the right, I took a photograph *[fig. 2]*. It was taken before the day light began to fade and the lights came on in the buildings at the far side of the road. Looking straight ahead, a shop window was to the side and in front of me *[fig. 3]*. At this stage there is no view to paint, just looking at everything that surrounds me. But the necessary outcome in the studio and the

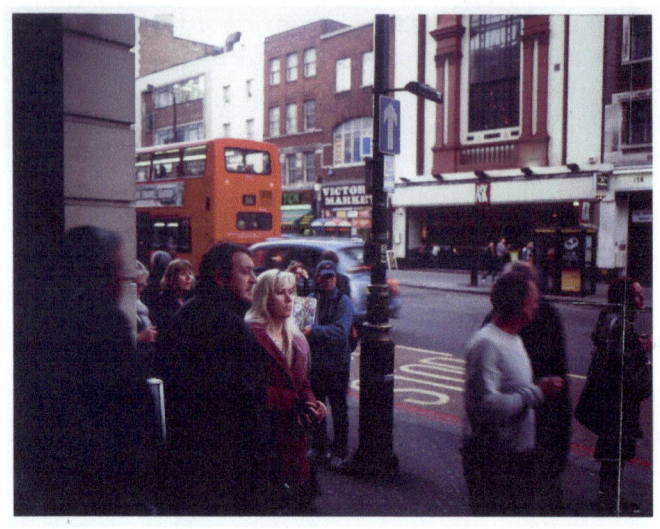

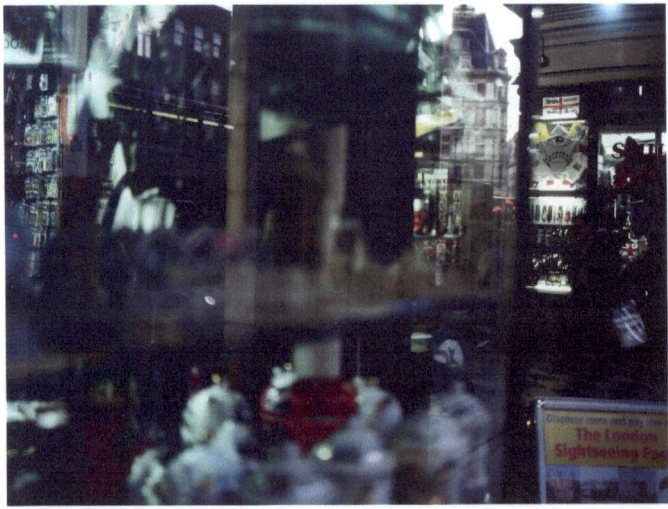

Figs. 2 and 3: Photographs taken to gather information for use in *Sun Setting Over Victoria*.

necessary state of painting is that all will become a view. That is a view contained within a rectangle placed in front of a viewer. But this view is an artificial construction of space. Its success is dependent on all its components yielding any other orientation apart from their placement within a spatial configuration. It is important not to confuse the views that art give us with the physical views in our world.

And when I returned to observing viewers of my work in Room 1 at the National Gallery, as I began to plan this new painting, I was reminded again of how, at the moment at which art achieves its autonomy and is a refuge from our world, my political engagement with the metropolis out on the street must be transformed into an aesthetic one. The people I have captured in the photographs do have a history and a future they are part of, and that will determine their meaning in our world. The opportunity to read the painting as a reference back to our world remains open to us, but as we do so we deny its validity as art and are regarding the painting no differently from the way in which we regard a photograph. But, whereas the photograph can only function in this way, with no unique status, the painting has been created to go beyond a narrative meaning, in which the world is not frozen, like a film-still, but achieves a stasis. In this state, there is no time-frame for narrative, but an ideal which perpetually asserts itself to the viewer (who is in a perpetual state of change). In this condition all that was political becomes visual. The people in the painting are out of our time and continue to assert their human *presence*. They will do so for ever. The only alternative to the stasis that art offers us is death itself, which is why art is so necessary to the human condition. I was fascinated by the comment of a very elderly lady who told me that all the people in my paintings were in a perpetual state of waiting. She enjoyed the exhibition hugely. The English have the term still-life, which is far more life affirming than the French *nature morte*.

* * *

The photographs taken at Victoria do not constitute any kind of template for a painting. They are not stitched together, traced or transferred to the canvas. In this, there is a clear break with photorealism and related activities, much of which fails to to find the uniqueness of art, typically existing either as a referent back to photography (and by extension back to our world) or the peculiar manifestation of a non-art process.

In the studio, drawing becomes the necessary means to construct art. This is always the case. Drawing is integral to the mechanics of art. This seems a simple statement, but a very important one to make at the present time. In the contemporary art world centred on the artist and not art, having the facility to draw is often cited in defining an artist. This is problematic because an artist must not only have the *capacity* to draw but understand the *necessity* to draw to construct a work of art. There are too many artists who can draw but eschew this responsibility, and in doing so relinquish their responsibility to art. Failing to recognise that drawing is integral to art is a failure to make art.

As art is dependent on drawing, my attentions are first to establish a tentative pictorial solution through small drawings. The solution invariably comes not from the location but is rooted in my previous experience of art.

A month before the exhibition at the National Gallery and my return visits to Victoria, I saw the realist exhibition at the Kunsthal Rotterdam. In a survey of art since Courbet, I was represented by my first painting of Victoria made a few years ago. I watched the way that visitors to this exhibition viewed my painting, which confirmed my own thoughts and I knew what I needed to do in future works. The painting is long, and the spatial configuration is stretched laterally, so viewers tend to look at the painting in sections as they move along it. It was a panorama of three spaces which just about held together but the energy of the work was being dissipated. It was too simple a solution to a highly complex experience. It reminded me a little of the way we laterally view a Pollock or the rather grander pictures of Charles le Brun in the Louvre. I needed to find a spatial solution which centred the diverse spaces, a tension which this painting largely failed to achieve.

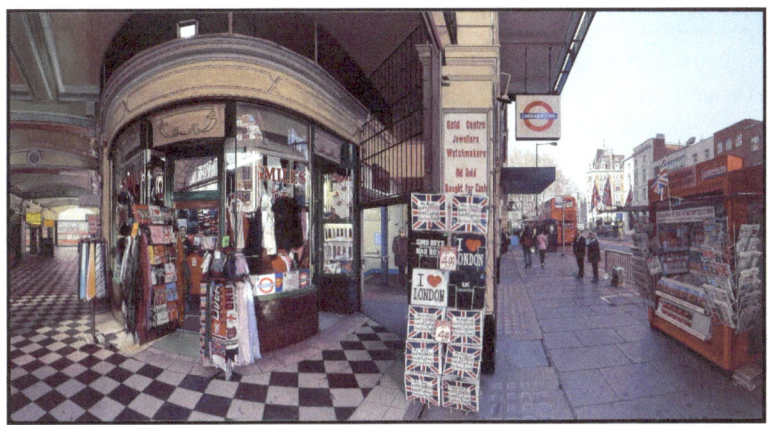

Fig. 4: Clive Head, *Victoria,* 2008 oil on canvas 169 x 302.3cm

I had found this in the second painting of Victoria, 'Leaving the Underground' but that was less concerned with a lateral arrangement of different spaces. The solution I hoped lay in the preparatory drawing. From the outset, I had planned to show the narrow edge of a curving shop window beyond the foreground window on the left, which could only be seen as I stepped to the right, and the view through the middle arch to the distant buildings and street beyond, which could be seen by moving forward and to the left. This began to build a more active central passage and the initial orthogonals were designed to focus the viewer primarily into the centre of the painting.

The term 'orthogonal' refers to a diagonal line receding into space to a vanishing point and is part of the nomenclature of perspective. I have now come to doubt the appropriateness of using the term perspective in discussing the construction of my paintings. It may well have become a corrupted term, referring solely to the simple geometric formulation of space which adheres to rules laid down in the Renaissance and reiterated through the mechanics of the camera and the algorithms of computer programs. This regards perspective as an existing formula which the painter uses to plot space. This would seem to be at odds with the necessity for each unique painting to determine its own mathematical configuration to achieve functionality. It also implies that to differ from the given rules of perspective is a deviancy as opposed to being crucial to the truth of the painting. In short, perspective has come to mean the space plotted by the fixed camera lens and that is of no use to me as a painter and probably has no use to any ambitious painter. We only have to look at the sheer invention within the territory of perspective prior to its fixing by Fox Talbot to see how painters used it with such creativity. In this state I am happy to discuss it, but now perhaps I should just refer to it as the mathematics of the space.

When Delaroche declared, on seeing the first photographs, that 'from now painting is dead' he might as well have been talking about how so much representational art made from then until the present day would be ensnared by the seductive space of the photograph. Prior to this fixing of the image, artists by necessity had to invent space and this spirit of

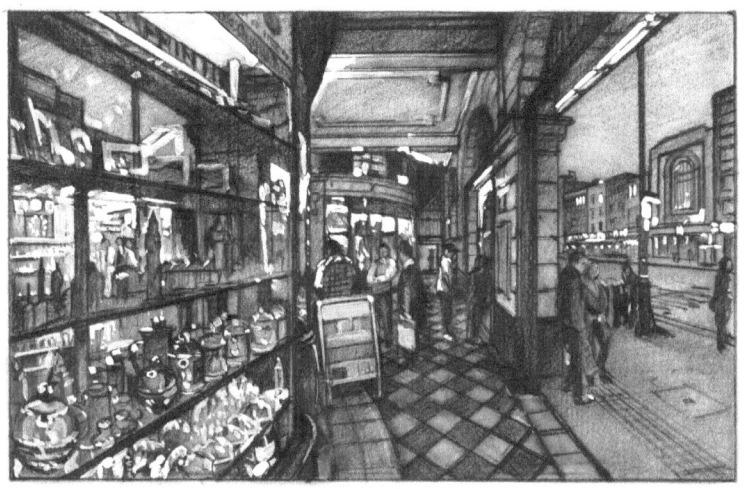

Fig. 5: Drawing for *Sun Setting Over Victoria*, 2010

invention lead to the hyper-complex strategies of Western art. But photography offered a ready made template for pictorial space, and realist painting, for the most part, adopted its spatial algorithm without question. In a very real sense, the use of photographic space by the painter turns painting into a readymade. Of course there was the remarkable invention of cubism, born out of experiencing the world as an active, participatory human being, but this was exactly the motivation for Titian, for Constable, for Canaletto, for Rubens, for Tiepolo and so many others.

In order to develop strategies for representational art in the future, the most fruitful source for artists to plunder is in painting made prior to the invention of photography. Here we may find artists using optical devices, but painting is always an act of creation from experience and simple beginnings and never a reduction from a pre-existing image. The depth and variety of human creativity on display at the National Gallery continues to make it the most relevant place for art students to study in the UK. But they must be equipped at the outset with the fundamental understanding that the purpose of art is to create alternative realities and the means to do this resides in the invention of space.

* * *

Now 'Sun Setting Over Victoria' is complete, I have begun to recognise the influences of two paintings in the National Gallery which I was looking at whilst my show was on. They are paintings I thought I understood before but they continue to surprise me.

Canaletto's 'S. Simeone Piccolo' was the subject of my impromptu presentation at a colloquium hosted at the beginning of the Canaletto exhibition, and the beginnings of my painting *[fig. 6]*. Central to my comments was the way in which it rejects the fixed geometry of perspective for a space that is elliptical. That is, instead of drawing the viewers attention solely into the centre and the far distance, Canaletto counters this by employing orthogonals to different vanishing points which keeps the eye moving around and across the painting. He finds a solution to the difficulty of a narrowing perspective that focuses the eye on a single point on the horizon which would result in the painting faltering into a stilted and motionless state. When we talk of the painting functioning , we are talking of its life force, energy and atmosphere. Canaletto creates this with a structure which is characteristically elliptical, lifting the viewer from outside the painting into and across a vast arena of space, the perimeter of which is marked by the buildings. Recognising this structure is how I would always recognise a Canaletto, and although we find elliptical space elsewhere throughout Western painting, Canaletto's orchestration is very distinctive. Seeing Canaletto against his rivals amply demonstrated this. In my own work I use many vanishing points, some of which cluster into 'vanishing zones'.

What is extraordinary is how the type of rhythm of orthogonals which delineate the profile of the city against the sky in the Canaletto finds itself running through my painting made when I was thinking about the Canaletto. That is, the profile of the buildings on the far side of the street and their reflection in

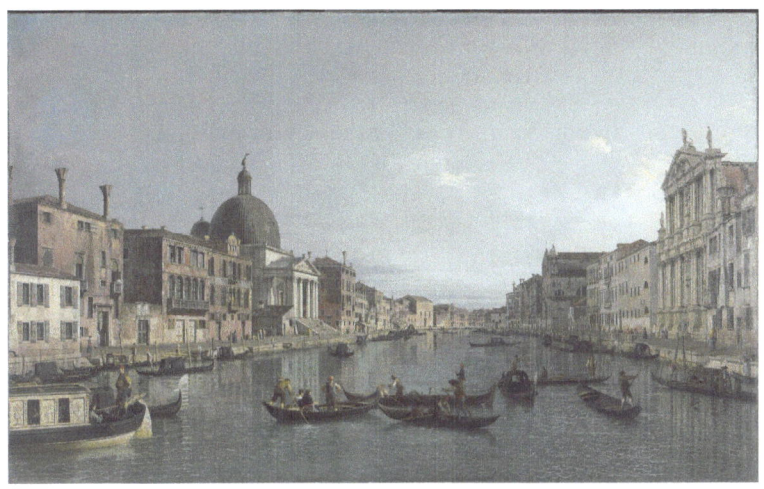

Fig. 6: Giovanni Antonio Canal, known as Canaletto, *Venice: The Upper Reaches of the Grand Canal with S. Simeone Piccolo*, 1738

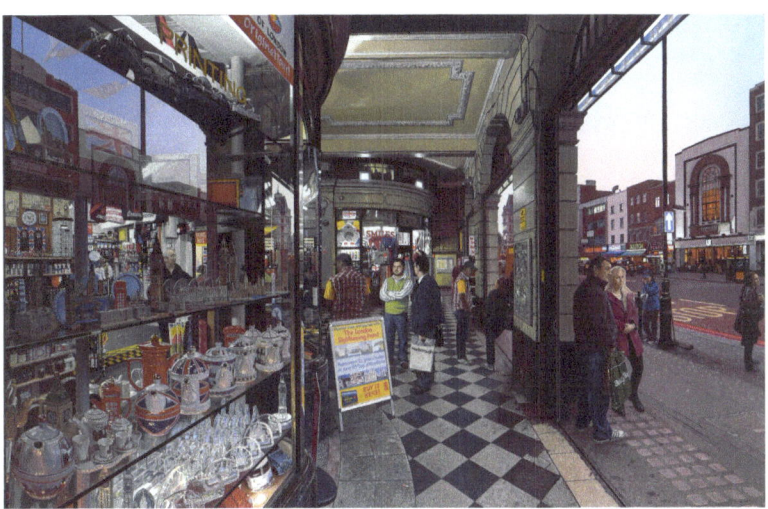

Fig. 7: Clive Head, *Sun Setting Over Victoria*, 2011, oil on canvas 134.8 x 213.9cm

the shop window create a gentle curve through the painting, which is very different from a conventional perspective that would rush the eye into the centre.

Despite the obvious formal parallels and an echo of the domes, this is not to suggest a literal overlay of form from one painting to another. That would be at odds with the creative desire to make something original, the desire to be an artist. More importantly the systemic nature of all paintings means that every part contributes to the function of the whole, which is why it is difficult to import predetermined formulas of any kind. It simply makes no sense to attempt to base the composition of one painting on a few formal attributes isolated from another. But it seems that in seeking a solution to my problem I have been inspired to use a kind of extraordinary spatial construction particular to Canaletto. Perhaps it was more a shared realisation. As I understood Canaletto, I intuitively understood what I should do, but I only recognised this when I finished the painting. It was part of the 'form knowledge' that is part of who I am, stemming from a long history of looking at work in the National Gallery.

It is certainly true that alongside the frantic experience of being on location at Victoria was the contemplation of a number of great paintings which have informed my painting. The second notable example being Poussin's 'The Adoration of the Golden Calf' *[fig. 8]*. The massing and rhythm of the figures have a similar relationship to my painting as that discussed with the Canaletto. It was not a conscious decision to emulate any of the groupings, nor is this really in evidence but there is some of its presence through the centre of my painting and the arrangement of figures against the rectilinear certainty of the monument/shop placed behind which stabilises both paintings.

Poussin's importance is his revelatory display of the construction of form and space. From him I have gained an understanding of the 'pervading light' of a painting which is at odds with the light of our world. I have set a light in 'Sun Setting Over Victoria' which is neither from the afternoon nor the evening light that I experienced. It is a præternatural light particular to the stasis of the painting, not the passing of time, though it is rooted in several hours spent on location.

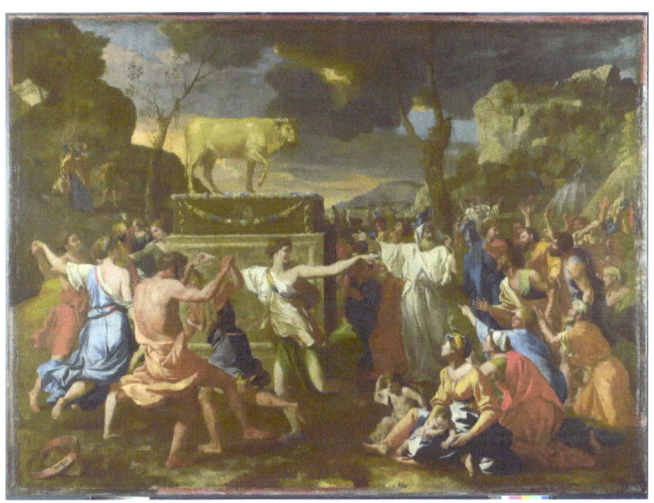

Fig. 8: Nicolas Poussin, *The Adoration of the Golden Calf,* before 1634

From Poussin, I have also developed a spatial construction that begins in the shadow of the picture plane. This sets the alternative reality well back from our world. This is not a *trompe l'oeil* painting, where the viewer is invited to physically enter the painting. Such paintings are curious extensions of our world, and like the more recent fashions for ready-mades, demonstrate a lack of faith in the unique existence of art itself. Such activity falters as being art because its meaning is based on functionality in our world, not its alternative. In painting, the point of such faltering is the surface of the canvas which is the boundary between the two states of existence. If the substance of a painting, its colour and tone are understood in their inert, absolute state and not in their position within the painted space, they have failed to be transformed from reality to art and are outside of art, no different from the existence of paint on the artist's palette. This is a collapse in the faith in art that we find in modernist formalism, where the mantra of truth to materials often lead to paintings as objects only in our world. But if we return to Poussin, it is so clear that colour and tone, for all their vividness, establish and sit within the space of the painting, and become its extraordinary light. His careful adjustments ensure that nothing sits on the picture plane and claims meaning by intruding into our world. I have described this as Poussin beginning his painting on a plane that sits behind the surface of the canvas, in effect, in its shadow. In my painting 'Sun Setting Over Victoria', this principle underpins the tone and colour, where every patch of colour becomes a patch of light. The temptation in a painting of extreme darks and lights such as this is to use the full weight of colour and tone available to the painter: black, white and colour straight from the tube. We would undoubtedly find this in a painting made by a realist who believed that art must mimic reality. But the realisation of an alternative credible reality render these absolutes largely irrelevant, as the atmosphere that will breathe life into this world can only be found *within* the parameters established by such absolutes. There are no blacks or whites in my painting or colours that have not been adjusted (and by default neutralised) to the pervading light. The visual field for painting is, in our reality, incredibly narrow. It is a narrow window through which we can create astonishing worlds. We are fortunate to have artists like Poussin to help show us this opening.

From the outset of making 'Sun Setting Over Victoria' I was conscious of drawing through a single line the form of an object and the space it occupies and demarcates. What is meant by such a simple statement can only be appreciated when looking again at Poussin, because here it is operating at a remarkable level. I likened his linear construction to the tectonic plate boundaries that make up the surface of the Earth, formed with such energy, which pull apart to reveal new territories. In Poussin's painted world, although objects might be regarded as conventionally overlapping one another, nothing feels that it is being obscured by that which is in front. That which is not shown simply does not exist and we accept this reality in a way that we would never do in our own world or in images of our world. And through his linear construction he opens up unique spaces, which then open up again revealing ever more pockets into which we can escape. Like tectonic plates moving apart, that spirit of opening space, and then opening again, through the firmness of the drawn line is something that I am trying to achieve in my new paintings, orchestrating ever more different spaces. In the past I might have compared this to Cubism, and its attempt to show us more and more, peering around corners. This comparison still remains apt, but the truth is we see this kind of invention reaching extraordinary heights in much earlier works.

All this now seems a very long journey from my activity outside the entrance to Victoria Underground, but if the sensory (or aesthetic) engagement with the place is a fundamental beginning, a new kind of aesthetic engagement in the studio is fundamental to the making process.

Drawing is both a mental and physical activity. It has a relationship to the body in space. This is the calm space of the studio in which each decision is given a physical and material form and judged on its presence on the canvas in this space. Drawing should be distinguished from draughting which has none of this physical interaction, and tends to be governed by known rules outside of the intuitive judgement of the artist. The computer is an appropriate tool for draughting, but drawing can only happen in a real space.

The contemplation that we talk of in the studio is one where thought is given material form. The end goal is to realise a unique material work of art and for this to happen the artist must explore through an interaction with materials in space. To make sense of all that has been experienced I prefer to be at a distance from the locations that provide my subject-matter. My studio is not in Victoria or even in a city. It is distanced from all that. The flimsiness of the transparencies and my flawed memories of the location compared with the permanence of the canvas fixed to the studio wall coupled with the solidity of the heavy drawn marks and weight of paint encourage me to be more inventive and less contrite in making radical changes to the subject. This takes place in the peacefulness of a rural retreat which could not be more different from the chaos and transience of the city. To find the resolution to the flux of the city I chose to leave it behind. In a bizarre paradox, I am reminded of the way Constable moved in the opposite direction, and found the resolution to the flux of nature through painting his greatest landscapes whilst in the city. This is a strategy for realist art quite separate from holding a mirror up to life.

At a certain point drawing activity is replaced by painting. Dealing with mass, tone and colour, and structural marks put me more in mind of the physicist, the engineer and the builder. There is no place in this process for the semiologist, and although at times I might become a sign-writer, the meaning of the words is their size, shape and position in space. The subject-matter is all that I have witnessed and *as an artist* I must make no decisions about the content based on narrative. However, I am highly selective. I reinforce the weight of each object through finding its essential structure and much is omitted that might clutter this certainty. I will chose and reconfigure into a single space a density of activity which actually occurred over a period of time. In my painting, the same person can appear twice as it is outside of time, and the reflection of a building can be in daylight, whereas in its appearance on the opposite side of the painting it can be lit with artificial lights. None of these things occur as a narrative on

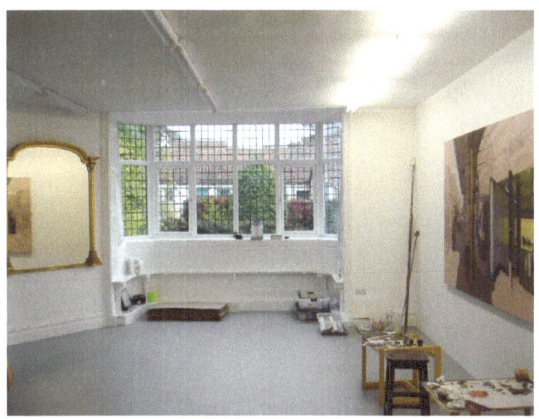

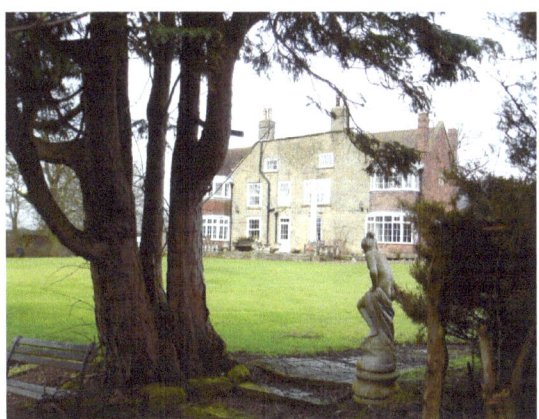

Fig. 9: Clive Head's studio in Yorkshire

time, but are solely based on the optimum visual solution. For the most part I am not even aware of such things until they are pointed out by others. They would only be anomalies if the painting is read as a referent back to our world.

In progress the painting begins to establish its credibility from the first few brush-marks. The authority of directional marks to create form and space remains the most vital tool for representation, far more so than any kind of lens-based media which is trapped by the homogeneity of its dull lifeless surface. But the spatial assertion of painting necessitates careful control if the final work is to be harmonious. Having established the means to create space far deeper than the photograph comes a challenging responsibility to create a unity through and around all that is presented.

The camera is a useful tool, and the use of photographs in making paintings will always influence the outcome. Whereas the relationship of photorealist painting to the photograph is omnivorously dependent, it is possible to develop a hyperrealist agenda outside of photorealism which places the unique invention of space and form at its centre, and at the same time recognises new pictorial possibilities thrown up by the camera's filtering. In this we might look back to Vermeer's obvious excitement in seeing the beads of light through the camera-lucida, and I attribute some of the sequences in 'Sun Setting Over Victoria' to curious visual effects in the transparencies.

But for a painting as complex as this sourced on a library of photographs which although large was of lousy quality, the process of painting is not made any *easier* because of the camera, it is just made *feasible.* Other processes are open to me and the painter Antonio López García continues to show us that it is possible to make hyperrealist paintings directly from life. But I choose to use the camera. I prefer to use photographs to remind me of how the objects would look if they were in front of me, and at the same time feel at liberty to simplify them and make them more solid because they are not. But at times I do paint from life, or just make things up as the needs of the painting demands.

The distance from the photography is shown in the comparison of the painted teapot in the lower corner with one of the source photos *[figs. 10 and 11]*. The configuration of the objects in this part of the painting has changed from how they appeared through the lens of the camera. The shifts in scale and the angles of the orthogonals are determined by the invented space of the total painting. From its beginnings the painting establishes control and I must follow its lead.

Partly mathematical but always judged by their material existence on the canvas and viewed in the studio as I pace around its space, each decision contributes to the functionality of the painting. In mundane terms this might be regarded as the establishment of form and space, but the consequence of this is the creation of a new reality and that remains the shared ambition of all true painters. The potential for this is always within the core of the painting and the skill of the artist is to make it a reality. The display of skill for any other purpose is outside of the remit of art.

Compared with the photograph of the teapots the painting of this area shows greater clarity and certainty. This is always the objective. The *alla prima* technique reveals that the means of representation is founded on the forthright application of colour through a directional mark resulting from a human gesture. From very small marks of this kind in evidence in Van Eyck to a more open and larger manifestation in Manet (which verges on the anarchic), this is the language of painting, but within it there is an extraordinary range of technique.

I have learnt to keep the surface of the painting varied and allow layers of colour to break through. The overlapping of marks is the simplest means to fix things in space. A drawn line may well be a boundary between forms and spaces but painted marks rarely abut; they are in front or behind. In my painting, this is reinforced by the use of a heavy lead white (flake white) which gives a greater density (a greater materiality) to each decision. In painting, it would seem that the creation of an alternative reality in which we can only mentally escape is brought into existence through a very deliberate physical and material interaction with our world both on location and in the studio.

In considering Poussin I discussed the purpose of his drawn line; the description of both form and the establishment of

25

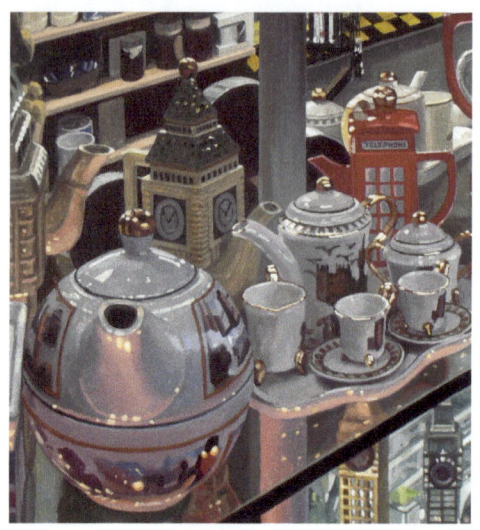

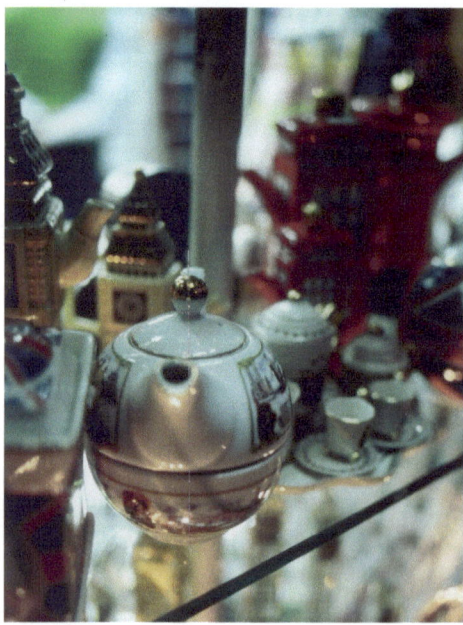

Figs. 10 and 11: Detail from *Sun Setting Over Victoria*, and original information photograph.

unique space. We can find a parallel duality in the painted mark, which must be locally descriptive but also be part of the rhythm of the painting as a whole. In my painting 'Sun Setting Over Victoria' its realism, or more aptly, its credibility, is not founded on a mimetic rendering of details using the smallest of brushes and brush-marks. Instead the painted marks must be part of a pattern across the painting. There is no place for tiny marks that would have no presence in this context. The units for this rhythmic pattern are varied in size but they must co-exist in a relationship which is as carefully determined as the juxtaposition of colours and tones. The credibility of the painting then does not reside in the details but the tension between marks, the scale of which relate to the human gesture (and the body in actual space) and the overall dimensions of the canvas. For this painting I not only wished to centre its energy, having recognised this as an issue in the first painting of Victoria, but also to crank up its intensity, painting on a smaller canvas and establishing a pattern of mark making which was denser than in previous paintings.

* * *

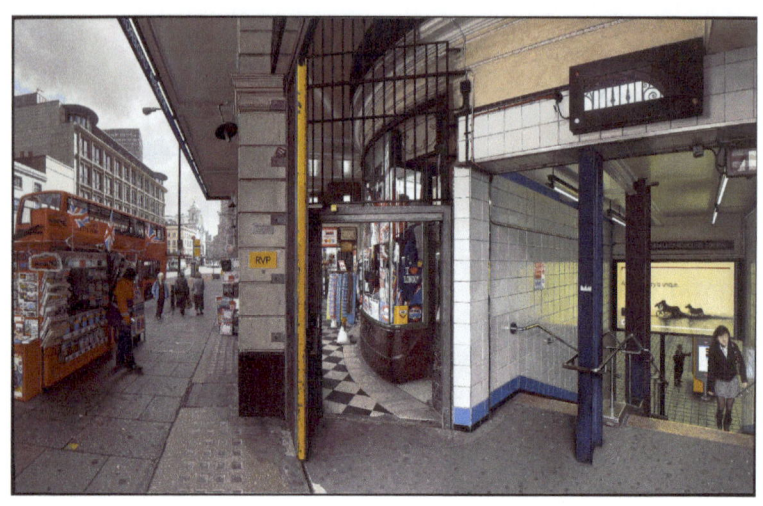

Fig. 12: Clive Head, *Victoria Underground,* 2010, oil on canvas, 149.9 x 240 cm

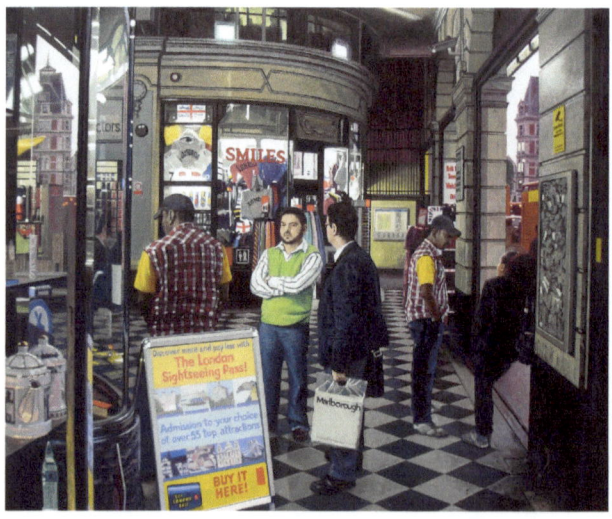

Fig. 13: Detail *Sun Setting Over Victoria,* 2011

The new painting was made as I was still coming to terms with its immediate predecessor 'Victoria Underground'. Based on the same location, but looking in the opposite direction, this painting also dealt with three distinctive spaces. Each of these was marked with a predominance of a different primary colour; red then yellow and blue. The coherence of its totality seemed to be rooted in a very classical, modernist framework. Colin Wiggins's comparison with Mondrian may well be appropriate.

It is always part of the decision making process to allow primary colour sequences to exist within the more neutral passages, all of which is held together with a pervading coloured light established from the outset. But the character of these sequences in 'Sun Setting Over Victoria' could not be more different from the solidity of the earlier work. The weighty masses of the new painting are in the darker shapes, the rectangle along the top edge, down the side of the column on the right and in the reflection in the shop window. There is a heaviness too in the arches, which reinforces a conventional classical space, not dissimilar to Giovanni Panini's 'Interior of St. Peter's' in the National Gallery. The primary colours, that is those that exist on the primary circumference of the colour wheel, the vivid reds, greens, oranges and most importantly, yellows dance across the painting in smaller, more varied shapes. There is a tension between what these little patches of colour represent locally and how they are liberated from mundane description and in turn liberate the rigidity of the painting. I am reminded of Dali's fragmented renditions of people and landscapes as he sought to illustrate the openness of atomic structures, but this is too simplistic. We can really find this kind of open rhythm in much earlier works, such as in Titian, where the whole is held together in a structure of coloured marks and shapes arranged across the painting. No less authoritative, this kind of structure breaks with the heaviness of more overtly architectonic solutions and in the work of such a master creates an amazing fluidity.

The central passage in the painting demonstrates some of this arrangement of primary yellows. The beginnings of each of these shapes is founded in the source material but the photographs have no such arrangement. Each patch of colour must describe but not be fixed too securely to the object. It is a careful balance and apart from the intensity of the colour and tone, there also needs to be an editing of information to allow the colour to find a level of autonomy. It is as if the journey that was set out at the beginning of this essay, from experiencing our real world to creating an alternative reality is being echoed within this invented reality, wrestling an independent reality for the painted shapes from within the painting itself. Not only does the delicate rhythm of these shapes remind me of the fractals that scientists describe in the natural world, existing in harmonies which defy simple formal analysis, there is also a layering of visual constructions which reveal themselves as we go further and further into the reality of painting, down to the level of the arrangement of the brush marks. It is the means by which art sets up its dynamic stasis, as opposed to the classical formulas which formalists from the last century were so keen to overlay.

* * *

The success of my display of pictures at the National cannot be measured by attendance figures or by reassuring the viewer that artists still have the skills to make realistic images. The greater purpose is to attempt some insight into the nature of painting and the relevance of the historic collection. That is more difficult to measure and it needs to be an ongoing pursuit in art education. It is a new aesthetic agenda which questions both the value of formalism and the misdirection of semiotics.

Painting is a life long pursuit, and with a little maturity comes the realisation that art is far more profound and, for all its variety, far more certain of its purpose than the chronology of 'isms' and issue-based agendas would have us think. They belong to adolescence as we try on conceptual frameworks because the real truth of art just won't reveal itself. But if we are not careful there is the danger that we will never understand and that society at large fails to understand.

As I continue to look at great paintings it is remarkable how they help me to develop my work in a relationship that simply didn't seem possible even ten years ago. There is a point where an artist begins to understand painting and perhaps is in a position to share some of this understanding with others. This is an exciting stage in my development because of the sheer joy experienced in viewing great works of art and the revelations that surface in my own endeavours in the studio. It is also a point of recognising that the factionalisation of art into historic and contemporary is unhelpful and may well account for the loss of any unique purpose to much art being made today. Collectively we need to acknowledge this situation and find ways to reconnect to art.

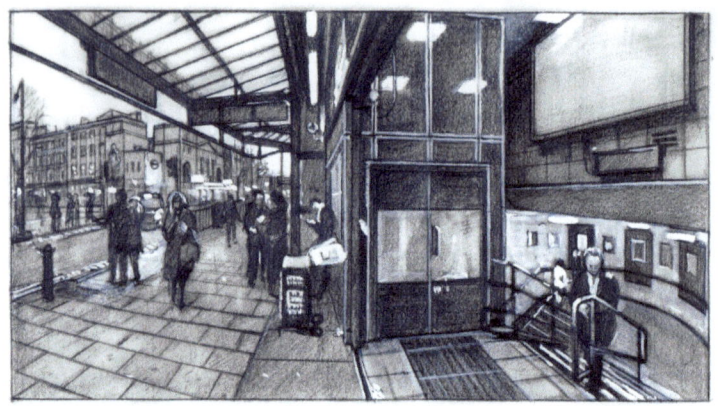

Fig. 14: Drawing for *Leicester Square Tube Station*, 2011

Also available from the Orage Press

Regeneration

by Michael Paraskos

Michael Paraskos is one of the new generation of art critics who are redefining the way we make and see art in the twenty-first century. He is a leading figure in the New Aesthetics movement, an informal grouping of artists and writers who emphasise the physical and material nature of art above its conceptual meaning.

In Regeneration Paraskos puts forward an argument for an aesthetic framework for art which does not look back to the academic aesthetics of previous centuries, but is rooted in the physical and material nature of how artists actually make art. By doing this, he suggests, an art theory based on the essential nature of art can come into existence, rather than a repetition of futile attempts to discuss art as if it is music, or poetry, or linguistics, or visual politics. Art is art, he suggests, and it does not need to borrow theories from other human activities to justify its existence.

But Regeneration is not simply a discussion of art theory. It is a record of a highly personal, and sometimes painful, journey into discovering the true nature of art. Originally intended for private distribution only to trusted friends in the art world, Regeneration offers a rare glimpse into the experiences that lead art theorists and critics to think, say and do the things they do.

ISBN: 978-0956580207

Also available from the Orage Press

Alfred Orage and the Leeds Arts Club
1893-1923

by Tom Steele

Alfred Orage was one of those mysterious figures in our cultural history who was in his lifetime extremely influential, and after his death almost forgotten. He was the co-founder of the Leeds Arts Club, possibly the only genuine manifestation of Expressionism in pre-second world war Britain, which promoted the philosophy of Nietzsche, the mystical socialism of the early Labour movement and suffragette feminism, as well as literary and artistic modernism. He turned the weekly newspaper The New Age *from a failing organ of the Christian Socialism movement into the British equivalent of Germany's* Der Sturm, *and the most widely read cultural periodical of its age. And he was the first mentor of one of the most important writers on modern art of the twentieth century, Herbert Read, helping to shape his philosophy of art, and through him the direction of international modernism.*

In this book Tom Steele follows Orage's career alongside the history of the Leeds Arts Club, showing that modernism in Britain was not wholly a London-centred affair. Whilst Roger Fry and Bloomsbury were following and promoting French modernism in the first two decades of the twentieth century, Orage and other figures associated with the Leeds Arts Club, including Holbrooke Jackson, Arthur Penty, Michael Sadler, Frank Rutter and of course Herbert Read, were engaged in the far more radical modernist ideas coming out of Germany, with Sadler even collecting paintings by Wassily Kandinsky in Leeds as early as 1913.

ISBN: 978-0954452384

.